Friendly Street
NEW POETS 15

§

Friendly Street
NEW POETS 15

A Lesson in Being Mortal • Louise McKenna

A Pause in the Conversation • Lynette Arden

Natural Intervention • Sher'ee Furtak-Ellis

§

Friendly Street Poets

Friendly Street Poets Inc.
PO Box 3697
Norwood SA 5067
friendlystreetpoets.org.au

Wakefield Press
1 The Parade West
Kent Town
South Australia 5067
www.wakefieldpress.com.au

First published 2010

Cover photograph copyright © Thom Sullivan
Cover design by Clinton Ellicott, Wakefield Press, and
Thom Sullivan, Friendly Street Poets Inc.
Typeset by Clinton Ellicott, Wakefield Press
Edited by Thom Sullivan, Friendly Street Poets Inc.
Printed in Australia by Griffin Digital, Adelaide

ISBN 978 1 86254 882 4

**Government
of South Australia**

Arts SA

Friendly Street Poets Inc. is supported by
the **South Australian Government**
through **Arts SA.**

Contents

A Lesson in Being Mortal
Louise McKenna
1

A Pause in the Conversation
Lynette Arden
31

Natural Intervention
Sher'ee Furtak-Ellis
61

Edited by
Thom Sullivan

A Lesson in Being Mortal

Louise McKenna

Louise McKenna was born in Rugby, England in 1969. She studied at the University of Leeds where she graduated in 1992 with a joint honours degree in English and French. In 1996 she qualified as a registered nurse before emigrating to New Zealand, then to Australia in 2003. She has had poems published in anthologies by Forward Press and was a finalist in the inaugural Cricket Poetry Award 2009.

Louise divides her time between her family and her occupation as a nurse. She is currently working on her first novel and a second collection of poetry.

Acknowledgements

Some of these poems, or earlier versions of them, have appeared in the Friendly Street Poets Newsletter and on the Cricket Poetry Award website.

Dedication
This book is for my family on either side of the equator.

Thanks
My husband Dave and my children for inspiring me;
friends near and far: Louise Hansen in Queensland;
Susan Arthure, Judy Garrard, Sue Mckone in South
Australia: Helen Cartner and Andrew Buddle in England;
Thom Sullivan whose editorial talents brought my poems
to life;
Maggie Emmett, Friendly Street Poets Convenor and skilled
poet, for her encouragement and support;
the brilliant poet Gillian Clarke who taught me how to
'kill my darlings';
and last, but by no means least, my grandparents, Peter and
Joyce Bloomfield, who first taught me the music of words.

Contents

The Queen's Pelican   4

Birds   5

Lemons   6

Feeding the Cassowaries   7

My Apology to You   8

Dragon Abreast   9

Visitation   10

The Knock   11

Bronze Whaler   12

8 Doomgate   13

Photo   14

Cone Shell   15

A Lesson in Being Mortal   16

Sonnet   17

Wicket   18

The Art of Absolution   19

Gallows Hill   20

Today's Music   21

Untenable   22

Encounter   23

A Drop of Water   24

Silence   25

The Ray   26

Journey   27

The Tracker   28

His Poetry Book   29

The Queen's Pelican

It isn't the eyes or the famed red-gold hair
crowning that autocratic Tudor stare
or even the borax and egg white
blanching the face

the numberless seed pearls inside the lace
of her gown
but something as natural
or unnatural as a monarch's frown.

It's the pendant weighing over her heart
a pelican stabbing at its breast
milking a ruby of its blood
to succour its young.

I see them often, pelicans
winging like pterodactyls
across the bight
over a seam of ocean. Then it is easy

to conjure myth. In reality, there is no blood
only a rancid, regurgitated pulp
fished from the mother's gullet for her brood.

But the analogy holds, like history –
how a mother often does
tear herself apart
for her children.

Birds

He could name most species:
a buzzard floating through Cornwall
or the latest migrant from Africa
and once, down under, he was surprised
by the rainbows on a lorikeet.
And he could twitter on *ad nauseam*
about swallows circling church steeples
and he hoarded misquotes from Shakespeare
concerning magpies.

And there was always the lone pair of tits
he would target in the sights of his binoculars
from behind his fence.

But he never liked the revenge
nor understood the equation of tits and milk
the foil on the bottle peeled back as cleanly
as the carapace of a beetle.

His cream knocked back long before
his cock ever woke him.

Lemons

I adore lemons:
bitter bombs of sunlight
make me salivate.

Feeding the Cassowaries

Through the diamonds of a fence,
their hands glued with sap,
my children are feeding the cassowaries.
Perhaps what fascinates the crowd
is this uncivilised glut
of quartered mangos,
the enormous kick of the throat
as the bolus of fruit passes.
Or is it the gaudy paint
of clownish blues and reds,
those inelegant tassels of extra flesh
or the strut of a gargantuan Jurassic turkey?
Blinking between absurdly large cilia,
as if focusing on the blurred grid
of their boundary,
it is almost impossible to imagine
the sudden helmeted charge
through a eucalypt thicket,
toes tearing at the viscera
of the boy who lost his way.

My Apology to You

comes gift-wrapped
like garlic
the packaging paper-thin
simple to remove
but the raw substance of it
is unpalatable.

Dragon Abreast
for Joan

Not the Shanghai River
but the Coral Sea.

You're out there in a bikini,
riding the leviathan's
map of skin
returning
from the *terra incognita*
of cancer.

And only you and your sisters can feel
the tug of her wings,
the great drum of her heart
sounding the deep as you beat
the thunder of each paddle.
A heartbeat away
from the toxins of jellyfish,
the healing motions of dolphins,
the sea as fickle as remission.
But the health of your anger
is constant.

Visitation

Last night on Middle Farm
he worked around the clock
for the lambing.

He found her when he opened
the barn. Startled by
the shock of the lamp switched on,

the lightning of her wings
ghosted right through him,
but all he felt was a silent rush of air

corrupting his hair and all he saw
was the aureole of the light swinging.
Later, down on his knees in the bloody

straw, between birth-rope
and faltering lamb, he saw
the evidence of her last meal,

a parcel of feather and bone
and he wondered at the way it dissolved
in the crux of his hands.

The Knock

When the timbers of that door creaked open
for the appointment you made with your boss
you felt like a guilty school child
looking up at a six foot cross.

Bronze Whaler

Look closely. She will do no harm
now the ocean has delivered her.
This shadow you have feared,
this recidivist killer
is now chained in sea wrack.
Come closer.
Those soulless, unfathomable eyes
will not see you,
the countless lancets
of her teeth no longer threaten.
Look at her snout.
That freckling of black stars
were sensors intelligently wired
to the shocked rhythms of life,
the electric agonies of death.

Feel her fins, belly and tail,
the preternaturally thick skin
has been vandalised
with scars and excoriations.
Look now,
as they turn her on her side,
before the coming tide rinses her clean.
Her blood as red as ours
from the unhealed stigmata
of the fisherman's spear.

8 Doomgate

Anything to escape your mother
and the price of your parents' charity,
corrupt landlord, local shanty of condemned housing.
For twenty quid a week, a dodgy, arthritic floor,
walls sweating salt-damp, the kitchen a suppurating sore
with its pus of green mould.
At least the toilet flushed
and the coal shed was cold enough
to store cheese and formula
and our bed was warm with three of us in it;
our baby curled between us,
while another was forming a question mark in my womb.
And that plot of garden was fertile:
when things got really dire you pulled up leeks for
        our dinner.

We stuck it out for months:
your parents' sulphurous sermons,
our sister-in-law wrinkling her nose up at our door.
Then one day, the landlord wanted his extra pound of flesh
as revenge for the unpaid rent. So we escaped.

Now after the remedies of distance and time
you see things differently.
This has not stopped you enjoying leeks.
And we laugh about it often,
Doomgate. The bruising irony. But sometimes
I still feel that northern chill, a sudden frisson
that travels to the bone when I remember
how our marriage, for a spell, iced over
like the pond in that garden
and how your parents closed in with skates on.

Photo

Whoever minted that description
of the eyes being the windows of the soul
is right.

Unlike the camera
they never lie. There is always
the glimpse of ruin, the glass of the cornea
revealing the ransacked house
and a flicker left in the grate.
The angry, sempiternal smoulder.

Cone Shell

Plucked from the jewellery box
of a reef,
painted perhaps
by mermaids,
folded like the labyrinth
inside your ear,
this shell will capture
the shunting echoes
of your blood
and convince you
that you hear the true notes
of an ocean.
You will never see
what lived
in its hidden sinus.
You will never feel
the harpoon's hook in your flesh
or suffer the slow glue
of its poison
stopping your lungs.
Its demon has been exorcised.
And it looks nice
next to the angel
on our mantelpiece.

A Lesson in Being Mortal

We thought we could weather this one
or stare it out in the beachfront café.
As we talked and spooned froth off our lattes
the sea began to boil. The sky dehisced its wound
and the suturing of horizon ruptured.
After a while, the ocean tested my nerves,
like the wall, each wave a seismic demolition of itself.
The path fast becoming water, a forensic pool of rage:
matted hairs of sea wrack, sponges scattered like
    brain matter.
And the beach, where we walked our dogs
and played cricket, was all sea.
The punters were a solemn congregation,
but the kids were squealing with rapture.
And when the sea tried to come in,
someone mentioned the storm of '48,
when the humerus of the jetty snapped
and the bone was tossed to the deep.

But for a time, we were fascinated,
the storm seemed to wipe out recession,
to wash blood off the pavements of Afghanistan and Iraq.
And I think it showed on our faces
how, once in a while, we are reminded that our lives
are like the mollusc we crush unknowingly underfoot
or the fish we see floating at the surface.
So I willed it to go on.

On leaving you pointed out the cormorant on a rock,
a soul islanded among the elements,
wings spread, as if preaching or praying.

Sonnet

Overnight, the geography of your world brutally altered.
The blizzard was like a god toying with a snowstorm.
    And now
you are miserable as it metamorphoses to slush.
    I imagine you
struggling to the supermarket, bent concave against
    the wind
like one of Scott's explorers. Here, we smoulder.
    Distances quiver
in the heat. Yesterday we found a fledgling dehydrated
    under a bush,
its beak gaping for water. After we syringed drops
onto its tongue and nursed it in air-conditioning,
    it survived.

I love the snow. Roseate twilights.
Untested lunar whiteness. Moth-flutter on skin.
That pillowy compactness creaking under foot. The way the
    world's acoustics
are muted and silence, trapped. But we are divided
over the seasons, as we are by the hemispheres
and destined to weather each inversely.

Wicket

for Joe and Tom

Today the outfield
is the Southern Ocean,
the wicket,
a gold sandbar.
What you glimpsed
in your camcorder's view
as a carmine bolt
of lightning
        is this delivery.
Now in replay
you can magnify
and decelerate
the ball's meteoric
arc and mark
its apocalyptic
        pitch.
And you notice the hunger
in the batsman's eyes
as he preys upon it,
slices it off the blade
of the bat, sending it
        into infinity.
Then you are shown
the fielder,
waist-deep in water,
arms pleading for a catch
and the elation slowly dawning
on his daughter's face,
as if she has captured
        a star.

The Art of Absolution

Today's headline:
a toddler abused to death.
Teeth missing. Father
turned the family Rottweiler
on him. Social workers had
visited nearly sixty times.
And I get an image
of Pilate, washing his
hands in a basin
of water.

Gallows Hill

I can still see the teeth,
the cured rags of fur clinging
to the cage of the skeleton. And I can make out those claws
that mercilessly tunnelled
into the land and risked
a farmer's patience.

The moles have been here for weeks now,
swinging like thieves
in the wind, barbed on their tree of wire.
They will remain here
until their punishment is complete,
until the crow and the buzzard
have taken the debased
mint of their eyes.

And I still see the guilty and the innocent,
herded, shackled, driven here,
strung up before the jeering crowd.
Parochial ignorance.
The ancient, uncivilised
sense of justice.

We had tasted it also, like the moles.
Although metaphorical, the torture
was as agonising
and all for something as benign
as digging our neighbour's backyard.

Today's Music

begins with polyphony
of Byrd-song. Then the *adagio*
of the kettle approaching the boil.
And the morning with *Classic FM*—
a suite from Telemann,
a rhapsody from Gershwin.
The finale of the morning
is the percussive clatter
of china in the sink
or the *staccato* of a text message
coming through. Then ringtones
on the bus, Midnight Oil, Men at Work,
remind you of how you used
to be cool. After school,
the familiar themes of *ABC Kids*
break that mid-afternoon slump,
before the quaint *entr'acte*
the washing machine plays
at the end of each cycle
recalls you to being a mum.

Later, on the way to the shop,
you hear the wind charging
the tuning fork of phone wires,
doves lilting in minor, a mellifluous sadness.
Then at the end, before sleep
you catch the brooding nocturne
of your heart pulsing in your ear,
perhaps the last music we ever hear.

Untenable

Both of them
were drowning.

She held on until she was aching
for air. Then she decided
to let her go, let the current whorl
its arms around her
until the jewel of her was lost
in the deep.

Afterwards, she swam
and swam, all the time afraid
of the leaking blood, a fin
slicing the surface.
She swam for her husband
waiting on the beach,
her sons building castles.

From now on, her sentence
will be the ocean itself,
the unforgiving silence of water,
the indifference of eternity,
where she cannot print
her name.

Encounter

Near the end of the jetty she hears steps behind her.
Until now, she has believed herself to be alone
on this island grafted onto the coast
and it is dawning on her how useful a weapon
a take-out coffee might be.
When she swings round
she discovers not a dodgy, hooded youth,
but a man of fifty years or more.
She makes that nanosecond appraisal
we all sometimes have to make – instinct versus reason –
and she notices how in the brilliance of the light
that the irises of his eyes are a harmless blue.
He apologises for startling her: it was not his intention.
Together they walk to the end of the jetty
where the ocean is everlasting and the night sky
is canted – an inverted bowl with a sugaring of
      constellations.
Then she sees how his face – like the dorsum of his hand –
is curiously unflawed, free of sunspots and wrinkles.
And his smoothly tapered fingers.
Pianist? Surgeon? She does not ask.
I live only a stone's throw away, he says,
indicating the coins of light glinting onshore.
He offers her that unblemished hand and it is
      strangely warm.
As he walks away, she turns back to the sea.
Far out, a light from a small vessel pulses.
Perhaps we are never truly alone, she thinks to herself.
Further along the jetty, a knot of gulls has gathered.
She is surprised she can no longer see him
and wonders why the birds never cried out
or scattered when he passed them.

A Drop of Water

beads
    from a broken tap
    in a city flat
spirals
    in the vortex of a plug
    down to the sluice gates
    of a sewer
dilutes
    his glass of *aqua vitae*
    etherises
    off his lip
ricochets
    down from a cloud
bounces
    off the cracked basin
    of the Murray-Darling
dissolves
    like saliva
    on the tongue
diffuses
    two atoms of hydrogen
    one atom of oxygen
    across the membrane
    quenches our thirst
drips
    cholera down
    the parched throat
    of a Mali infant.

Silence

is the fantasy of the telephonist
and the woman packaging CDs
in the cacophony of machines and machines.

And the sounds we can't stand to hear:
the tinnitus of traffic
or the Messerschmitt drone
of a mosquito homing in on your ear –
that goading assault on the auditory nerve –
make us yearn for a fraction of peace.

But there is a difference
between silence and peace.
The former, created.
The latter, given.

The woman in aged care,
patronised, wiped, muffled
by a blanket, she will tell you
the meaning of silence,
after the lights go out.

And the man alone on the beach
or the dog howling
in the empty throat of the house,
they hear the prolonged hum
of nothingness, the white noise
as cruel as Beethoven's deafness.

God, give us peace.

The Ray

I dig hard with the paddles.
Through the fibreglass eye of the kayak,
filmic scenes
of a swaying lost kingdom
bloom into view.
I watch as the eye
passes over limestone gorges,
forests of seagrass,
deserts of corrugated sand.
A jellyfish spiriting out of a valley
gently steals my breath.

Suddenly, he is there,
right under the kayak.
Out of the nimbus of sand
he has created
I see him now in front of me.
I paddle for all I'm worth,
just in time to see
his neon-sprinkled skin.
But he has sensed me
and is gone, faster than
water buries light.
And a sudden emptiness —
as if God had just risen
and walked away.

Journey

The tram is not unlike
a hospital waiting room –

that enforced, undiscriminating
proximity to another.

I might be sitting next
to an accountant, a cleaner

or a psychopath. But we are all
ultimately heading

in the same direction.

The Tracker

Before he got his burns
he painted.

So we arrange for acrylics:
intense white, ochrous browns,
cobalt blues
and a canvas to
be brought in.

After a day
he shows me the emu's tracks
across the desert.

His Poetry Book
for Susan

You lent me this book. It is one of those beauties
that punches you in the gut
because it is poetry.
And when I open it, something else
viscerally wallops me – your words
scripted on the flyleaf,
a private dedication to your husband.

I read the poetry. And I knew why you'd
chosen it, for its nacreous shine,
although it delivered the most cataclysmic of slaps.
And your words to your husband,
they are poetry because they are true and entrusted
and as potent as Shakespeare or Heaney
or Yeats or this earthiness from Durcan.

And I know you would agree
that poetry is the diagnosis
that packs the above-mentioned punch
or breaks our heart
makes us laugh in public places,
palliates us like a cup of tea,
betrays us like the crash of empties
in a recycling bin
or sensitises us to pain.
And after the bellows of the lungs have relaxed,
the valves of the heart have stilled,
what remain are words.

A Pause in the Conversation

Lynette Arden

Lynette Arden was born in Sydney and brought
up in country towns in North and Central Coast
New South Wales. She completed Honours degrees in
Geography (UNE) and Graphic Design (Liverpool
Polytechnic) UK and has lived and worked in Australia,
Papua New Guinea and the United Kingdom.

Living in Adelaide since 1979, Lynette now works as a
volunteer for a number of organizations. From the 1990s
she designed and painted murals for local libraries and
Adelaide Zoo, where she works as a volunteer. She runs two
workshop groups for the Adelaide University of the Third
Age and designs and runs websites for a couple of
community groups. She also designs and sets up small
publications for several community groups.

Photograph courtesy of John Barnet

Acknowledgements

Some of these poems, or earlier versions of them, have appeared in: *Treasury of OzPoet*, *The Mozzie*, *Valley Micropress* (NZ), *Eucalypt A Tanka Journal*, *paper wasp*, PoetWorks Press (USA) anthologies (*Just Bite Me satire, whimsy and other tasty treats*, *A Nickel's Worth of Dreams* and *When I was a Child*), Poets Union anthology *Ask the Rain*, poetry.about.com anthology *Poems for Peace*, *Writers on Parade*, *Taj Mahal Review (India)*, *Ribbons: Journal of the Tanka Society of America (USA)*, *FreeXpression* and the Adelaide Zoo website. One poem has been broadcast on *891 Evenings*.

Thanks
Members of the following groups have given me generous support and advice:
Kensington and Norwood Writers Group, Bindii (Japanese form poetry group), Friendly Street Poets, Society of Women Writers South Australia, Adelaide U3A Writers Group and the former Writing Right group.
I also thank members of several Internet Forums for their help. In particular: OzPoets (now archived), where I started to learn what poetry was about, AHA Poetry Forums and the mentors of the World Haiku Club workshop.
Thank you to Graham Rowlands, who gave valuable advice on structuring and editing my submission and also to Ann Timoney Jenkin for her advice and support.
Thanks to Ron Heard, editor of *The Mozzie*, who first encouraged me to submit work to publishers and to Beverley George, publisher of *Eucalypt A Tanka Journal* and previously *Yellow Moon*. Her advice and encouragement have been invaluable.
Numerous individuals have given me feedback on my poetry. Thank you to them and also to the world around me for inspiration.

Contents

My Flesh   34

Glamour   35

Glossy   36

The Twenty-five Most Beautiful People
in the World   37

Tanka and Haiku   38

Sepia Memories   39

Girl Child   40

Brief Encounter   41

Tigers   42

Tiger   43

Memory of Murano   44

A Good Age   45

Unvarnished   46

Departure   47

Tanka   48

Early Morning Images   49

Waving   50

Frieze   51

Her Garden   52

I Hang On   53

Haiku/Senryu   54

Haiku   55

Weightless Words   56

Fall   57

The Game   58

Whither   59

My Flesh

The glass of my life
is seven eighths full
and my flesh is made
from the ashes of stars.

The air that I breathe
is drawn from the breath
of billions of lives
and the wind from the south.

The water I drink
has circled the earth
frozen as ice, fallen as rain
and wept as the tears of prophets.

The food that I eat
has been grass and worm
and the laugh in my mouth
has been heard in the dawn

on the frost bitten grass
at the foot of the ice.
I painted the mammoth
on the cave wall.

I threw the spear.
I chipped the axe.
I carved the needle.
I carded the wool.

The glass of my life
is seven eighths full
and my flesh is made
from the ashes of stars.

Glamour

In the department store mirror,
lit like a glamour queen,

I try my new Poppy King lipstick

and it's *Hello Marilyn!*
Goodbye Norma Jean!

Glossy

photos of Brad & Angelina
& Tom & Katie & Nicole

no stories about William or Harry
or even Charles

just Princess Mary smiling
at unsmiling orphans in Senegal

and people dressed as cupcakes
not in the recipe section

which seems to have gone missing
it's all takeaway nowadays

salon staff dressed in hipster minis
chrome everywhere

the hairdresser has cut my hair
just like Posh Spice on the front cover

Gel? she says.

The Twenty-five Most Beautiful People in the World

This morning
at the supermarket register
there are the Twenty-five Most Beautiful
People in the World
including me and the checkout chick,
who has a slight acne rash
and a big yellow badge with
red writing which says
Happy Easter.

None of us is buying the magazine.

Tanka

early mornings
she would sit and knit
woollen cardigans
I still wear
mother's arms around me

Haiku

in a high window
a light winks out . . .
starlit night

gathering acorns
under the tallest oak
autumn wind

Sepia Memories

The shadow of my father
falls on a wilting patch of lawn,
his back to afternoon sunlight.
Aged two, I hold a peach,
frown into sun, serious,
small legs in firmly buckled sandals.

Sepia conserves those days.
The peach has long been eaten
or thrown away;
the sun has disappeared
below the horizon, risen and again set.
We have donned new clothes
many times over, held flowers,
smiled into lenses,
been snapped in different poses,
flattering, unflattering, alone, with friends,
or trapped at inadvertent moments
with smiles misplaced, hair blown by wind.

Of all those printed memories
to me most poignant,
in front of a small girl
in large sunbonnet,
the shadow of the photographer
caught in that moment.

Girl Child

My mother taped my ears back
so they'd be flat and neat.

My mother curbed my flights of tongue
so I'd grow up discreet.

My mother stayed impetuous hands
forever slamming doors.

Now here I am, a little Gem,
or a tiger without claws.

Brief Encounter

She arrives
in a cheetah spotted coat
hair a blonde ruff
eyes as innocent
as kitten's fluff.

His face shines, eager.
Her eyes narrow
as if to brush
imaginary crumbs
from a furry cuff.

Later I see them leave.
His hand caresses her sleeve
and the car purrs
while she stores,
snapping the glove box,
a spare set of claws.

Tigers

summer day –
seeking a glimpse of tigers
we fall silent
at a distant roar
splendid and terrible

Tuan
moves among grass
stripes
rippling in smooth play
of flesh over muscle

Assiqua
pauses at water's edge
lapping
her reflection wrinkles
through sky and clouds

Kemiri
streaked ebony and sunlight
blends
into drowsy noonday
dreams with no boundaries.

Tiger

Kemiri,
beautiful one,
I wait where
striped ink grass shadows
slide into amber pools
drowning in clouds.

Kemiri,
who is the breeze flowing
through grass stems,
dozes in the hot sun.

Kemiri,
tawny eyed,
stretches as the sun sets
pads through the forest
paces the twilight.

Kemiri,
when you prowl
even the wind pauses.

Memory of Murano

Shook crystal catches bright sunlight.
Again I see the fire glowing;
I hear the ferry chugging past
the islands of the dead.

Again I see the fire glowing,
the artisan intent on form,
the islands of the dead
dark in the cave of race memory.

The artisan, intent on form,
draws out a curved glass animal,
dark in the cave of race memory
or another trinket for tourists.

He draws out a curved glass animal,
a bull for the dancers of Mycenae
or another trinket for tourists.
The salesman's teeth shine white in his olive face,

a bull for the dancers of Mycenae.
We Italians all bargain.
The salesman's teeth shine white in his olive face.
Smiling he dangles the necklace.

We Italians all bargain.
I hear the ferry chugging past.
Smiling he dangles the necklace;
shook crystal catches bright sunlight.

A Good Age

That's a good age, ninety-two!
What's good about it? she mutters behind the door,
you'll be there soon, the way the years go,
you'll be there soon or gone before.

What's good about it? she mutters behind the door,
welcoming the visitor with a sweet smile.
You'll be there soon or gone before,
she considers privately, all the while

welcoming the visitor with a sweet smile.
I preferred the age of five, myself,
she considers privately, all the while
she shuffles slowly, walking for her health.

I preferred the age of five, myself,
parties, dresses, presents and games.
She shuffles slowly, walking for her health.
It is hard to skip when in your nineties, on a frame.

Parties, dresses, presents and games!
A few oldies round for a cup of tea and scones,
it is hard to skip when in your nineties on a frame.
We'll sit and strain to listen, hearing aids on.

A few oldies round for a cup of tea and scones.
You'll be there soon, the way the years go.
We'll sit and strain to listen, hearing aids on.
That's a good age, ninety-two.

Unvarnished

You heard about Don?
I say.
Found dead in his house,
I say.
Five days he lay there,
I say
nobody knew.
The wood bench is still there
where he quaffed his beer.
The van didn't take it.
Relatives didn't want it,
unvarnished, a bit like Don.

Departure

This is the departure lounge;
from here we go into the dining room.
Some of us think we are going home.
The weather along the corridors is fine.

From here we go into the dining room;
wheelchairs are stacked in an alcove.
The weather along the corridors is fine.
Through the windows we can see rain.

Wheelchairs are stacked in an alcove;
we sit in silence to eat our meal.
Through the windows we can see rain;
I'll have a nap straight after lunch.

We sit in silence to eat our meal;
the food is bland to pamper our digestion.
I'll have a nap straight after lunch.
The dining room is rather quiet.

The food is bland to pamper our digestion.
We only have a short walk from our rooms.
The dining room is rather quiet;
quite a few of us are losing our memories.

We only have a short walk from our rooms;
some of us think we are going home.
Quite a few of us are losing our memories.
This is the departure lounge . . .

Tanka

this map
of flat blues and greens
I fold up
into cliffs with crannies
holding flannel flowers

my feet
scuff tide-line foam . . .
a puff
behind the steamer
crawling the skyline

Early Morning Images

first sun
between the pickets a geranium
glows

ruffled cypress
full of honeyeaters
singing

coral tree branch sways
into rising sun
rosellas shriek

garbage truck flourishes
a rain wet bin
red lid swings

asphalt glitter winks
heels clatter past
my hello

Waving

the breaking wave holds its secret
under the slipping edge

the mirror surface
declares foam and sky
in the holding of one breath

then the vivid slice
of the surf ski

Frieze

five teenagers in the mall
flip through a Sunday afternoon

the turning edge of the skateboard
mixes boredom with anticipation

this is the typical part of a crowd
on an ancient frieze always

on the verge of breaking
into disorder, the sculptor

still sketching the scene
before taking up his chisel

Her Garden

My neighbour removes her plants
if they don't perform:
too spindly, flowers too few,
untidy, tendency to droop.
She layers them in piles, roots up
to die of asphyxiation
or dehydration.

All in the garden
must be long of limb
and full of bloom
or compactly clumped
and flower for months.
In her garden
I would have been weeded out
long ago.

I Hang On

I hang on to something familiar
in a place where everything changes.
Even the bluebells last only a moment.
In the spring garden rain is falling.

In a place where everything changes,
except the days which now seem similar,
in the spring garden rain is falling.
In my thoughts all is in movement,

except the days which now seem similar.
My visitor makes tea and rearranges.
In my thoughts all is in movement.
I press the buzzer. They are stalling.

My visitor makes tea and rearranges.
I sit in my chair, feeling grimmer.
I press the buzzer. They are stalling.
Through the window the sky is in ferment.

I sit in my chair, feeling grimmer.
I have no friends here. They are strangers.
Through the window the sky is in ferment.
I will walk on my frame in the morning.

I have no friends here. They are strangers.
Even the bluebells last only a moment.
I will walk on my frame in the morning.
I hang on to something familiar.

Haiku/Senryu

fading daffodils –
once again he rings
her answering machine

quiet morning –
the cat inspects the blue
of the lizard's tongue

old dog minding old man minding old dog

Haiku

drought
a fallen leaf curls
over its shadow

garden path
ants bring tiny shadows
into the sunshine

country road
dogs bark at speeding
dust clouds

Weightless Words

I picked at ordered
trays of letters,
laid down metal phrases
with a printer's fingers.
I inked the block of type,
ran the heavy press,
dried the crisply printed sheets.

Now I stare at weightless
words in cyber light,
ghost words:
easily written,
easily wiped.

Fall

Miss Hedge aims the spray can
thoughtfully, reflectively
at the stream of ants swarming
over the windowsill.

From the back of her mind echoes
Exterminate! Exterminate!
and there were the Saturday papers
so much killing and torture.

What is to be done? she murmurs.
Some of them have wings.

Sunlight flows over the sill, warming.
A vine leaf spirals downward
in the still air.

Her finger tightens
on the button.

The Game

This is the end game.
We read it in the stars.
This is the play without name.
We are mere cat's-paws.

We read it in the stars,
again there will be war.
We are mere cat's-paws,
no umpire to mark score.

Again there will be war,
after destruction, famine,
no umpire to mark score,
show us we are human.

After the destruction, famine,
earth littered with mines.
Show us we are human.
Give us some sign.

Earth littered with mines,
fields sown with salt, stones,
give us some sign,
leave us flesh to cover bones.

Fields sown with salt, stones,
this is the play without name.
Leave us flesh to cover bones.
This is the end game.

Whither

The year commences.
Unprocessed refugees
set fire to desert prisons.
There is more talk of war
and argument about the justness of causes.

Bright sun reels
over the Barossa,
flushed with last year's vintage,
plumping out this season's grapes
on rows of gnarled vines.

The young, leaving home,
rush about on country roads,
throwing up dust,
speeding down highways
towards city lives.

I sit and listen to the radio
and dig about in old books
for a new beginning.

Natural Intervention

Sher'ee Furtak-Ellis

Sher'ee was born in Elizabeth Vale, South Australia, in 1976 to a Polish-Australian refugee and a preacher's daughter from Port Pirie. Her first job was as a checkout chick. Since then she has had more jobs than roast dinners, so she has gathered a wide range of skills and met some amazing people along the road.

Sher'ee was educated at Elizabeth Downs Primary School, Craigmore High School, Marden Senior College, Comskill, the University of South Australia and learnt the most important lessons from the 'school of life'. She has earned a Bachelor of Arts (Honours) in Communication Studies, majoring in media production.

Acknowledgements

Some of these poems, or excerpts from them, have appeared online at www.bipolarpoetry.com and in *Mad Sad Words*, edited by Dr. Joseph Dunn (2006).

Dedication
I would like to dedicate this work to my aunty Nora Weaver, bravest of the brave.

Thanks
Thank you to Friendly Street for giving me the push-start! I would like to sincerely thank my sweet husband, my family, my extended family, my metal mates, my soul brothers and sisters and everyone who has ever come into my life and made an impact.

RIP: Maria, Dorothy, Reg, Grandpa Bob, Des, Laurie, Dad, Lynda, Sam, Barry and Brenda. Gone but never forgotten.

Contents

Drought	64
Seasons Inside	65
Lead to the Clinic	66
A Work in Progress	67
Distant Cousin	68
Say Goodbye	69
Firefighting	70
Eternity	71
Corpses	72
Rebel	73
Madeline	74
Paper Moon Town	75
Living the Life	76
Big Man	77
Old Songs	78
Balloons	79
Journey	80
Potential Section 269	81
Water	82
Empty	83
Glass Case Detachment	84
Heartnotes	85
Tired	86
Texas Bar Brawl	87
A Black Cloud Covered the Sky	88

Drought

The drought has hit.
A thirsty rodent wanders the dry streets
cares for nothing but a drink
dodges his untimely death by breathing slowly.
A drop of someone's spittle falls into his open mouth.
It will save him.

The Great Southern Land is yellow, tan and green
but mostly wrinkly, old and obscene
disaster has struck this country.
What can the crocodiles do?
Where will the kangaroos go?
Does anyone know?

Saltwater and green eyes
and suddenly a tear
from a cactus in the desert
so warm from the heat
the sun is making her thirsty.
Here we shall stand and celebrate
when the water finally drops upon the land
the result of our hysterical bawling
and the cascades will be bursting.

Seasons Inside

In autumn the tree branches twirl together
like two bodies in love
cuddling, holding their own among the dirty and
    dying leaves.

In summer a dry wind blows through my damp hair
cooling skin as red as wine
the sun is generous and divine.

In spring the wonder lights up my heart
bringing colour to the most bland
like bright pink nails on a soft, pale hand.

In winter I layer our love in warm sheltered hugs
it's freezing and dark so we gather close
celebrating kindly the life we chose.

Lead to the Clinic

My hands usually have *lead* pencils to use
with rubbers to erase the blues
write a note, I will, then watch it disappear . . .

The medicine bell rings loudly
just swallow, then lie in your room and wallow . . .
in a cell with misery and memories
they give you apples – and fruit is good for fruits!
But I never saw a *lead* pencil for me to draw
not even in the charts on the door
we had temporary pens to write a ransom note
played with big bouncy balls
and two-string guitars that were funny to see.
But how can we play them industriously?
Have you ever had boiled chicken? she asks,
because generally it should be roasted or fried or grilled
    or barbecued.
No way! Not in this place. It usually comes out in a mask!
Just stay out of the way, José!
and keep your yoghurt in the back of the fridge where no-one
    can see.
I gallop like a horse back to my stable
I will never eat at their tables again.
Everyone else in the pig pen is a pig!
What did you expect, stupid?

Back on the farm
my hands have *lead* pencils to use once again
with rubbers to erase the blues once again
write a note to the generic food for the last time, I did
then watched it disappear . . .

A Work in Progress

As the wind blows, we sit and think about love and death.
What's the difference, he says, *you lose your soul in both cases?*
I don't agree, I'm thinking you're a cynic.
Let the wind blow, I reckon, *the breeze is good for some.*
Our foundation is almost the same.

If I love you so much, then why do I hate you too?
Was it the place we were stuck in
or my face in your view too much like you?

I walk upon this sacred site and you curse me
just like you did all those years before
I'm so sorry, I was just a stupid kid, a little baby
scared, angry, hurting for vanity, creating insanity.

If you loved me so much, then why did you hate me too?
I now know that the place we were in was skewed
too much to view, I'm so much like you.

So I'm here now, away from you
it's never the same to be alone without you
there's no-one to honour thy Father
like offspring left grieving.
We never forget how much you loved us
we're sorry for the growing pains.

If I loved you so much, then why did I hate you too?
Was it the place we were stuck in
or the face in your view that was too much like you?
I shouldn't have said that, should I?
Too much like you.

Distant Cousin

Hey you, how *you* doin'?
slip under my eye
I never thought
I'd find my equal
in a place like this
asphalt and diesel
dry as the desert
the grey everywhere
nothing but everything like school
but people are similar
we soon become
familiar faces
wanting to leave
but missing the dirt
the rats and roaches
so to my cuz I beg
help me get out
this ain't my thing
no verve for me
I need to see trees
and colourful beings
don't try to protect me
my shell is resilient
the path is to test
life is the reason
I know you mean well
but only I know best.

Say Goodbye

Goodbye to the light and hello to the night
say hello to the moon, to the sky
I hear that dreams
never seem the same when they become real.

Wild sparkling red wine
curse the gifts it gives
time time tick tock tick tock got no time
curse the lack of it, why bother with the shit!

Say hello to the wretched morning light
bid a foul-mouthed farewell to the night
say goodbye to the man in the moon
and the black star-filled sky.

Dreams will never be enough for you
don't succumb to fear, it won't help anyone
give your tears, sweat and blood
it's only a nightmare.

Goodbye dreams, hello sky
goodbye light, hello night
goodbye moon, fair and square
farewell.

Firefighting

Whizzing, whirling, the air is so naughty.
Twisting, turning, the world is on fire.
Sizzling, burning, the trees are scorching.
Front-ways and backward, the animals cry ...

I can't stand the heat
can't live much longer
can't see my sisters ahead
can't breathe this smoke anymore

Cutting, chopping, the leaves are mulching.
Jumping, running, we leap through the flames.
Higher, longer, the saints on the mountains.
Spraying, staying, till night becomes night again ...

We can't fight in these smelters
can't see in deep orange light
can't feel anything but hot walls
can't go on, we must get *out!*

Sitting, waiting, wiping sweat from her face.
Eating, drinking, our hunger is sated.
Stretching, crouching, we wait for our call.
Clicking, speaking, the radio tells us to run ...

No, no I cannot return, I am not a hero
I can see what I'm doing here
so yes, yes, I can go on, we must go on, we can go on
this is our mission ... to fight.

Eternity

There's a place in the country
where the tree always stands
the leaves fall every autumn
the ground never cracks
and the grass doesn't die
even in the harsh heat of summer.

Will you come and visit me beneath the sturdy tree?
It will forever cover the sun off the hallowed land.
A cemetery lies between
the golden leaves and luscious green,
but have you ever wondered how the grass still grows?

When do the parasites start digging in
and the dead become a shell of bones?
Why can't we dig them up, replant them and start again?
Even if he doesn't look the same
can I grow him back just like the sturdy tree?
Put him in a planter-pot and water him each day
give him top-grade soil and feed him *Thrive* and hay?

We hate the absence, but it won't go, it fades.
I wish I could stop the rain, so it will never soil his new
    home again.
Mud on the fallen leaf and on the grave.
No more weeping, nothing can bring him back.
Accept the fact,
he's rotted and black.

Corpses

Lost in his soul, he'll never grow old
a man in his prime forever
skeleton in the ground, a sacred mound
wreaths and flowers all around
his name on a stone, a carcass in its new home
the mourners stand alone

Where is his spirit? We all want to know.
Did the devil get him or did he float to heaven?

Curse the evil that remains on this earth
for the devil should have them instead
it's funny how they live in glasshouses
wear blessings around their necks
the hypocrites continue to lie
while the good people die

Angry at God for taking your love.
Why does he need them, if he sees that you still do?

Rotting corpses
were once here
rotting corpses
no longer there
rotting corpses
what a waste

Rotting corpses
stink!

Rebel

everywhere the rain stains
dry up and be grateful
once you were a stream of pure
now you've become so hateful

everywhere a pot of gold
cheer up and just take it
you used to be a practical angel
now you'd only waste it

yes wind will blow your hair
humidity will ruin your make-up
heat will fatigue you
cold will bite you
and yes, the hail will hurt you

everywhere the pain stains
grow up and be grateful
once you had a dream of pure
now you've become so hateful

no it will not last forever
it will not ache constantly
it won't be you alone
and no, nobody will know.

Madeline

Madeline spoke and everyone listened
she wasn't much to look at and her voice didn't glisten
her words weren't important to anyone great
but someone decided that good fortune was her fate

I want to scream at her
and shake her by the head and wake the bitch up
she is not an angel and she'll never be a saint
but the substance within her will set her free

Madeline the intellectual, read academic books
when others snickered, she just gave dirty looks
there's nothing that really upset that girl
unless someone she loved was in pain or hurt

I want to scream at her and tell her how imperfect she is
slap her humble face
remind her that all good 'guys' die young
I bet she won't care, she's left her mark here

Madeline, I ask you to teach me how to be
respectful and successful and happy
you are the one who lives as she pleases
I am the one the whole world teases

So I poured out my heart and pleaded for aid
from the girl who knows everything
and you know what she said?

AARRRRRGGGGGGHHHHHH help ME!!!!!!!!!!!!

Paper Moon Town

No way known I'm going back
the Northern plains are a remnant of the past
under the ground, mounds of bones from those who loved
    and lost
the paper moon town contains the dreams of weary dwellers

How come the sky is always blacker at night in the
    old land?
Fear is instilled in the minds of naughty and nice children
a dry backyard, a fruit tree or two among the weeds
the paper moon town could never hold me back but always
    holds me down

A face has been drawn on the paper moon
with a big grey crayon or charcoal stolen from art class.
Is it mine?

Occasionally I see comrades from the old land
who have come full circle and seen the future too
some have exceeded their dreams
but mostly there are those who drill the craters
because the paper moon town taught them this is all they
    can do –
I refuse.

Living the Life

The soul will cry, tears in coke
the soul will sigh, no more hope
the heart will mourn, hide the dope

Where is your heart?
Where is your head?

The soul will die, blood on dirt
my soul will fry like oil is burnt
the soul will lie, you're such a jerk

Where is your hand?
Where should it be?

The soul is gone – who fucking cares?
her heart will roam and cats will stare
peace will never come to a person so ill
never a day will be perfect and still.

Satisfaction? Pride? Happiness?
Thanks for nothing.

Big Man

I know I'm not supposed to feel this way
I did not know you as long as they
still I was your friend
each day till the end
I yearn to find the tears
to grieve those two lasting years
I miss your warmth and smile
to talk for just a while
eat lunch in style
a Milo in the aisle
makes me happy today
and all the other days
because I felt like an outcast
and you made me feel welcome
part of something real
thank you for your precious time . . .
Dude.

Old Songs

Old songs
make me bleed

Old songs
haunt you and me

Old songs
never leave us, just die

Old songs
turn their eyes away

Old songs
a bark-bird on the ground

Old songs
beauty in a sound

Old songs
feel familiar and free

Old songs
with love we used to see

Old songs
trusted then betrayed

Old songs
in the end all fade.

Balloons

Yesterday, I was a deflated balloon
cut open wide
beaten again
floating back down to the ground
crushed through the thin ice
blood everywhere
I don't care

I'll make it

Today, I'm a floating balloon
on a windy day
pushed and pulled
yanked from my favourite place
strangled by ribbon
blue in the face
I'm fucked

I'll make it

Tomorrow, I'll drift away
into a cloud
not that I'm allowed
but I'll fly
fly far away

I'll make it!

Journey

So confused, but so sane
so normal, yet so insane
learnt but not taught
hurt but can't fight.

Scared it will come running
frightened of the corners of my eyes
listening to hear what I don't
hearing the lines you speak.

Same feelings in every cycle
stay focused on the view
light up the night road
Hell awaits my burning heart.

Scurry to nothing, nowhere to go
sobbing and sighing, healing the rage
love is what I'll never know
however, I may understand.

You pray for a sign, a message, a voice, a guide.
Who will give you all the answers
and show you the way to a brighter day?
Life will be the way *you* want it to be.

Potential Section 269

So tired
and dizzy
yet cannot sleep
not allowed to yet
must adhere to the regime
although you are not in prison
you have not committed any crime
but you could be considered an offender
forced to endure this trial until your soul expires
eating away at your skin and bones and nails and hair
until liberation day arrives in your hands on the way to town
it walks amid my dreams and between daily journeys of labour
however, it seldom appears and pays no interest so is it even worthy?
What do you think or care? Are you brave enough to intercede? I implore you!

Water

The flowing depth of undue rain
river, stream, floating me further
soft and cold, liquid gold
master of human existence

you could be shunned
O Mighty One
rigid texture, tastes so fresh
wet my inner life

we pray for rain
dear Mother Earth
to end the pain
the drought brings

this one could end
your fair deliverance
ungrateful minds and bodies
not sufficient to survive
empty, dry souls
        would slowly, slowly die.

Empty

the man feels no sorrow
the man feels no pain
the man runs off to the next city of sin
and gives up faith in vain

the man feels no sorrow
the man feels no pain
the man wakes up alone one morning
and decides to *plan* his fate

he watches scenes from glass
he hides behind an ego
he stands above and starts to worry
with thoughts of love betrayed

the woman feels like crying
the woman sensed his loss
the woman grieves
until she snaps and leaves his face beyond

she steals a wink and smiles
she answers quite sweetly
she dances with unfamiliar shadows
that claim to care deeply

they will show us the world these boys
ending your life after a heinous race
a few tricks and turns in hotel rooms
she runs back to base to repair her face

Glass Case Detachment

elegantly wasting time
stranger waits in sublime
blowing harsh yet calm till dawn
strangely feel my fingers torn

just don't want to leave
self determined heave
fantasy world deciding
isolation is inviting

seven ways to know
if evil owns your show
so if it's my lie and my life
return to me my knife

taste the eager sucker
hunger for some ice cool
attraction to use her mind
yep, he's just not my kind

although the dream subsides
you won't satisfy my ride
for now she could say
tomorrow talk, no way!

Heartnotes

Feet, keep walking
hands, stay focused
face, tell your story
legs, jump those obstacles
arms, let's hug.

Everything is just as it seems
no broken dreams
when working as a team.

Mind, be sensible
spirit, get lucky
stomach, the truth is here
heart, stay beating
bones, march smoothly.

Faithfully we embrace the view
no need to fear
we'll just take our cue.

Tired

When I fall asleep in a crumpled heap
a weary paper bag
and I haven't even taken off my shoes
there's nothing left to do but sigh . . . and she does.

When I leave home for more than a comb
like a butterfly
and I can tell you aren't gonna be fun
maybe I should run . . . and I do.

When I speak of horror and it shocks you
like an electric chair
and you can't face the burns
let's see if we can work it out.

Take pride in psychotic perfection
your animals become your life's attention
was that too much to mention?

Life looks so rosy from there
let's just stay right here
we don't need anything else
zombies live in plastic peace.

Texas Bar Brawl

White skin
purple from the beating
lying there waiting
shining my eyes upon you
seeing you quite clearly
the blade enters deeply
quickly removed you start streaming
and then you are gone.

Darkness blankets us
watching shadows move around
riding my pipeline
clouting the stomach
sharp edge silver fishing blade
darkness blankets me
living returns.

Nasty fucking whore, martyr to the core
kicks a man when he's down
curses the whole town
triumphs in evil, causes a sight
psycho ex-wife armed with a knife
delivers her rage
pummelling under bear-hug blunder
drops to the ground
ex drives around
party stopped by cops
gather round the mops
blood stains on the porch –
luckily no corpse.

A Black Cloud Covered the Sky

As I step onto the train
I can smell their pain
I want to run away
then I hear them pray
like we're going to find a way
in all this disarray

I glide into the grey
I hope somehow he'll pay
for the sins of the day
I know I have to stay
to help my mother on her way
as the tapestry starts to fray
the light's been taken away
I try not to let my head lay
but now I begin to fade . . .
'a shvartse khmare hot dem himl batsoygn.'*

*'a shvartse khmare hot dem himl batsoygn' –
'a black cloud covered the sky' (Yiddish)

Friendly Street New Poets Series

Friendly Street New Poets 8 (2002)
The Windmill's Song · Elaine Barker
Kite Lady · Tess Driver
Fine Rain Straight Down · David Mortimer

Friendly Street New Poets 9 (2003)
Peeling Onions · Jill Gloyne
Crescent Moon Caught Me · Judith Ahmed
Scoffing Gnocchi · Linda Uphill

Friendly Street New Poets 10 (2004)
Stealing · Libby Angel
Deaf Elegies (from Virginia Woolf's Record Store) · Robert J. Bloomfield
Sparrow in an Airport · rob walker

Friendly Street New Poets 11 (2005)
low background noise · Cameron Fuller
words free · Simone G. Matthews
jars of artefacts · Rachel Manning

Friendly Street New Poets 12 (2006)
The Night is a Dying Dog · Steve Brock
Travelling · Margaret Fensom
Nectar and Light · Murray Alfredson

Friendly Street New Poets 13 (2007)
Black Magic · Courtney Black
Circus Earth · Janine Baker
Hieroglyphs · Roger Higgins

Friendly Street New Poets 14 (2008)
Snatching Time · M.L. Emmett
The Boy Full of Broken Promise · Rob Hardy
Airborne · Thom Sullivan

website: friendlystreetpoets.org.au
email: poetry@friendlystreetpoets.org.au
postal: PO Box 3697 Norwood SA 5067